Thomas' Little Light

Patricia Beth Rodgers

Illustrated by Romy Vekony

Thomas' Little Light

Copyright © 2017 Patricia Beth Rodgers. All rights reserved. No part of this book may be reproduced or retransmitted in any form or by any means without the written permission of the publisher.

Published by Wheatmark®
2030 East Speedway Boulevard, Suite 106
Tucson, Arizona 85719 USA
www.wheatmark.com

ISBN: 978-1-62787-401-4 (paperback)
ISBN: 978-1-62787-402-1 (ebook)
LCCN: 2016935634

This book is dedicated to
Pastor Roy Smith and his wife Mary,
the Sunday school teachers, and
the loving congregation of
Lawler Baptist Church
near Florence, Texas.

*This book is dedicated to
Pastor Roy Smith and his wife Mary,
the Sunday school teachers, and
the loving congregation of
Lawler Baptist Church
near Florence, Texas.*

Table of Contents

1. Missing Daddy 1
2. Sunday Trips to Lawler Baptist Church 5
3. Letting My Little Light Shine 9
4. News About Moving 13
5. Welcoming Daddy Home 17
6. Walking Your Pig 21
7. Riding an Elephant 24
8. In Search of a Mystery 29
9. Acting Out Plays & Riding in the Magic Bus . 32
10. Playing Baseball & Hunting Deer Antlers . . 37
11. Talking to Dear Lord 41
12. Three Little Pigs on the 4th of July 45
13. Leaving County Line Ranch 50
    The Real Kids 57

Chapter One

Missing Daddy

Daddy left for Iraq just before summer started, like he'd done four times since he and Momma married. Momma said she'd had a new child to look after each time Daddy left to go to war. This time was no different. Leah, our older sister who lived the first seventeen years with her own momma in Tennessee, came to live with us at County Line Ranch. That made Momma responsible for four of us and her patience was worn pretty thin. As the only boy in the household, you'd think I ought to get the most attention. Wrong. But, thank goodness Mia, my constant companion, shared my love for cowboys, guns, and boots, or I'd have gone nuts surrounded by all of Abby's Barbie dolls. For my little sister, I'd always be grateful.

Besides living in a house full of girls and having to share Momma's attention with all the others, I felt like I had plenty to whine about this summer. For one thing my growing pains were really bad. Often I would feel the leg cramps coming on and jump out of bed and rouse Momma at night. She'd assure me that they'd quit hurting soon enough, but snuggling up against her on Daddy's side of the bed always made me feel better. Sometimes when I'd exasperated her with my whining all day, I'd pull my trump card of pretending to have a bad case of growing pains just so she'd hug me and quit being mad at me. It would have been nice to have Daddy around to wrestle me down and tickle me silly.

Mia missed Daddy terribly. She'd be saying her Dear Lords at nighttime or in Granny Pat's van just before our county road hit the highway. Right in the middle of "and please keep Daddy safe, and don't let him bleed or get hurt." she'd stop and sniffle and ask, "Where are you, Daddy?" With a little prompting from me or Granny Pat, she'd finish with a little sad "amen" and Granny Pat would pull out onto Hwy 195 and start her Dear Lords.

Abigail missed Daddy, too. But, she'd been through this three times before and knew he'd come back and call her his princess once again. She kept herself busy with her Barbies and a closet full of Tinkerbells or somebody-else fairies. Movies were one of her favorite pastimes and we'd stand in her room and cheer for the good guys and shoot the bad guys. Abby was great about telling the good guys from the bad guys. She'd promise the bad guys that they were going straight to the hot water where the Devil lived. I liked it much better when she talked about how we good guys were all going to heaven where God lived. The hot water really scared me.

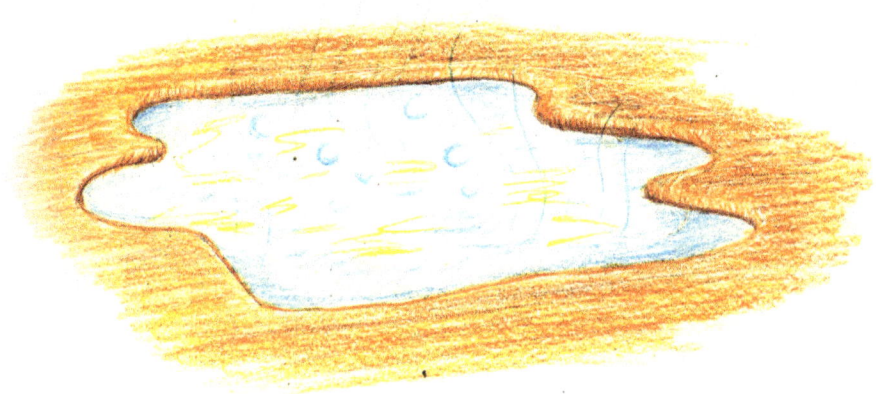

Leah was mostly quiet. I wondered if she would talk more when Daddy got home. Momma was heck bent on Leah passing every one of her classes at school so she could graduate with her class of 2012, so Leah did a lot of studying when school started. Leah caught on to my baby act of whining for attention shortly after she moved in. She would look at me and say, "Really, Thomas?" She wasn't interested in playing cowboys and Indians with me and Mia. I figured she was too old to know how to pretend.

My granny Pat never quit knowing how to pretend. She could come up with a story almost as fast as I could. Her biggest joy was to make us costumes and write a play that had a part in it for each of us. She bought every one of us a scrap book and made stickers to match our many costumes. Every time we performed, we got to put a sticker in the book for each person in the audience. Always there was a line or two in the plays that talked about God or Jesus, so we could call our book a witnessing book. She thought if we started telling others about Jesus when we were young, then we could fill every page by the time we went off to college. To me the story about how Jesus died for our sins was easy, and I couldn't figure out why everyone didn't learn it when they were little. I guess they didn't go to Sunday school at Lawler Baptist Church.

Chapter Two

Sunday Trips to Lawler Baptist Church

We went to church every Sunday morning with Granny Pat and Grandpa. One morning, Abby stayed at home with a sore throat, so only Mia and I went with Granny Pat. Grandpa always took his own truck because the noise we three children produced inside the car made him bonkers. We'd already made the left turn off the highway and driven by Mrs. Caskey's concrete pigs where we stopped and I counted them correctly for Mia. Mia said there was twelvey of them. The pigs still had their red bows on from last Christmas, but we didn't mind because we knew Mrs. Caskey didn't get around as well as she used to. We liked to stop and have our pictures made with the pigs and Mrs. Caskey's blue bottle tree. Sometimes we even got to go inside and tell her hello.

After the pigs, but before the ranches where we counted the horses and told which color of horse we

wanted to ride when we grew up, Granny Pat said, "Oh, no!"

"What's wrong?" I asked.

"What's oh, no?" Mia asked.

"Someone ran over a squirrel. He's lying dead in the middle of the road." She quickly added, "But don't worry. He's already in heaven running around and eating pecans."

I spoke right up, as I knew that wasn't true. "No he's not! He's still lying back there on the road!"

"Wight, Granny Pat. Da squirrel's on the road!" shouted Mia, always the one to mimic whatever I said.

Right then, I got my first lesson about the invisible thing living in your body called a spirit. It's your spirit that gets to go to heaven and have all the fun with angel wings. Your old body doesn't get to go, and I felt pretty sad about that and wondered if maybe we shouldn't ever tell Abby that story 'cause it'd make her too sad. Abby liked her pretty Princess body and would probably want to take it with her to heaven. Maybe someday when she was eleven, we'd tell her.

After we counted horses and I'd picked out the paint one and Mia a black one, we went on to Lawler. Mia and I marched right into our Sunday school rooms and told everyone hello. Both of us used to cry when Granny Pat would go off and leave us, but we grew up real fast and learned that the Sunday school teachers were nice. They didn't ever yell at us or send us to timeout. They just wrapped their arms around you, hugged you, or they'd pick Mia up and rock her. Sometimes I wished Momma and Granny Pat could teach Sunday school as they'd be much nicer to be around if they did.

After Sunday school, Granny Pat came to get me and I had to go into the church and sit on a pew beside her. We sat on the very last row because Grandpa said it would be easier to drag me out by my ear if I didn't behave. I knew he was just talking scary and so did Granny Pat, but just to be sure, she made him sit on the row in front of us. My grandpa has a bad habit of teasing me and making me holler. Maybe Brother Roy should talk to him about that.

Granny Pat showed me how to find a number in the music book that matched the one in the white menu. She sang really loud, but Grandpa just patted the back of his pew.

I held Granny's hand when it was time to visit with everyone around the church and I shook a few people's hands. I felt kind of crushed in a couple of places 'cause everyone was so much taller than I was when they stood up. I liked it better when they were all sitting down and we were even.

Grandpa took up the money in a round wooden plate. When it came down our aisle, I put in my dollar bill and Grandpa's folded check. But before I turned it loose I noticed everyone else had their check wide open with the writing showing, so I took the time to open up Grandpa's. Since it took me a little while to get it open, people turned to look. When I got the check just right and looked up, they were smiling at me. Embarrassed, I tucked my head up against Granny Pat and stayed that way until the good time started.

Chapter Three
Letting My Little Light Shine

The good time was when Brother Roy got up to preach. That meant I could have my candy I'd gotten at Sunday school and open my dinosaur sticker book that Momma had sent with me. Before I had one piece of candy all the way chewed up, I had twelve or fifty-five dinosaur stickers stuck on my clothes and on various places on my body. Granny Pat finally put a stop to my sticking when she saw me push one onto my forehead. Seeing the mean look in her eyes, I peeled off the stickers and placed them in the dinosaur book. I was thinking maybe I should talk to Brother Roy about Granny Pat's mean eyes.

I paid attention just enough to hear Brother Roy say we all had a light to shine. None to quietly, I leaned up to Granny Pat and asked, "Where's my light?" Without taking her gaze off of Brother Roy, she patted my chest. I didn't want to cause a disturbance and tell Granny Pat that I didn't have a flashlight sewn into my shirt like I did the lights

in the bill of my camouflaged cap, but she shushed me. Then I heard Brother Roy talking a lot about sin.

"What's sin?" I asked in my quietest voice.

Granny Pat whispered that sin was doing something you knew better than to do. I asked if it was like Grandpa teasing me all the time and she rolled her eyes and said no . . . But she said to be quiet and we'd talk about it later. What was it with old people? Why didn't she just tell me she didn't know? I'd understand. Why, heck, there were lots of things I didn't know about.

Brother Roy had something white in his hand and I asked what it was. Granny Pat said it was a big tissue, a handkerchief. He seemed to be crying and a lot of people got up and went up near him and kneeled down, but nobody stopped to speak to him. Were they mad? 'Cause his voice was shaking and it made tears come to their eyes.

He said at the nursing home a little lady in a wheelchair asked him why she couldn't go on to heaven and I think he was upset that he couldn't take her there himself. Granny Pat whispered that he was talking about her momma, Granny Mac. I wondered, too, why God wouldn't let Granny Mac go to heaven. Was it because she never got baptized? Maybe I should ask Abby about it. Abby knew all about baptizing and going to heaven. All of her millions of Barbies have been baptized zillions of times.

After the candy was gone and the good part of church was over, I asked Brother Roy at the front door where my light was. He did the same thing Granny Pat did, pointed to my chest and said right there. I thought about it on the way home and decided my spirit must have its own flashlight so it could see around inside my body. I hoped the batteries didn't get wet when I got baptized someday as

Momma was always warning us about ruining our batteries. Hey, maybe this meant I could skip baths to save my spirit's little light. I'd ask Momma for sure about it tonight when she said to take a bath.

When Daddy got home, I'd have a lot of questions to ask him. One I'd ask for sure was how did he keep his light from burning out while over in Iraq. It must be hard to recharge his battery when he was so far away from home. Maybe next time at church, I'd just ask Brother Roy to pray about that.

Chapter Four
News About Moving

I liked listening to grownups talk. I pretty well understood a lot of the parts that they didn't spell. Grandpa didn't spell anything, so I hung around him the most. Momma claimed he was a good influence on me since he never cussed or seemed to get mad and say things that shouldn't be heard by little pitchers with big ears. Really, though, she liked it that Grandpa took me out of the house and away from Mia 'cause Momma was worn out of hearing one or the other of us holler, "I had it first!"

A little while back, I heard something that made me scared. I was pretty sure Momma said our family was going to leave County Line Ranch next summer. Next summer sounded like a long ways away, but what did I know about time? As far as I could tell, Monday mornings came every other day and Saturday hardly ever came around. Summer might just slip up on us pretty quick and off we'd be gone.

The reason we'd be leaving was Daddy made Sergeant Major of the Army and he needed to go to a school where they could teach him something else about being a soldier. That made no sense to me as he already knew how to aim, shoot, and clean his gun, so what else would a soldier need to know?

I cried when I went to bed that first night after I heard the news that we were

moving. Just thinking about leaving home and going off to some scary place we'd never been before conjured up some really bad things. What if the boys there were all big and I was small? What if we couldn't take our toys and I had to leave my transformers here? And what about Granny Pat and Grandpa? Who would help Grandpa feed the cows and help Granny Pat herd the white rabbits into the pen at night if me and Abby weren't here to help? And Mia, what if there were cars everywhere and she didn't stop when Momma yelled at her to stop and she got runned over?

The next morning it occurred to me that I'd worried for nothing, 'cause I remembered that Daddy wasn't even home from Iraq. For sure we couldn't go without him. Knowing that Abby couldn't hear real well, and that she would probably go berserk if I told her we had to move, I decided to

keep the news to myself and try not to worry. Just to stay on top of what was happening, each time I found Momma talking on the phone, I hung around listening. But her conversations were about as long as it took to drive to Kiki and Granddaddy's house in Tennessee, so most times I wandered off and missed a lot.

Then I overheard Granny Pat talking about Mike being home soon. Did she mean my daddy? When I questioned her about it later on when she was reading us a book, she said he would be home sooner than he'd been gone. In other words, it wasn't going to be as long 'til he got home as it'd been since he left. I understood her perfectly, but Mia couldn't figure it out. She wanted Daddy home now, that very minute, and started crying that she wanted her daddy. Patience was pretty hard when you were little, I guessed, but I really couldn't remember back that far.

    I asked Momma when daddy would be home and even though she didn't give me an answer, she smiled the biggest smile I'd ever seen on her face since Daddy came home last time. I was pretty sure that smile meant that he'd be coming home pretty soon . . . Yet, how could I be happy about him coming home if we'd have to go with him to that new town called El Paso? For the first time in my whole long five years of life, I wanted to be alone, and I ran out the front door where Sarge, Grandpa's dog, tripped me up and I went sprawling across the board porch. When I went back in, crying about the tiny skinned place on my knee, Momma couldn't figure out why I was carrying on so.

Abby says when you're upset about something you should talk to someone about it. So maybe I should tell Abby we were going to have to move and she could wave her magic princess wand and make it not so. Or maybe, since she was a good witch at Halloween, she could stir up a happy syrup that we could both drink that would make us invisible and we could hide when it came time to move. But, no, I couldn't tell Abby, as change was hard for her. She'd get it stuck in her head that moving was bad and until next summer came around, that was all she would talk about over and over again. I best keep it a secret until someone big decided it was time to tell us. Maybe by then I'd have figured out how to keep our family on the ranch.

In the meantime, I'd just act real happy when Daddy got home. Actually, I would be really happy Daddy was home so I'd just pretend to be sad that we were moving. But, you know, it was kinda hard to pretend to be sad because we were moving when I really didn't even know what moving meant. Maybe El Paso was only as far as the other end of the ranch. I could nearly almost walk that far in a day and Granny Pat could drive there in less than a minute. Moving like that wouldn't be very hard as I could probably just hang out a lot with Grandpa and not even notice much that we moved.

Chapter Five
Welcoming Daddy Home

Daddy came home two days before Thanksgiving! Momma snuck him into the house the night he returned and hurried us off to school the next morning with Granny Pat. Daddy went to Leah's high school that afternoon and surprised her. Then the three of them, plus Granny Pat, drove to mine and Abby's school to surprise us.

The entire school was in on his secret and all of the classes from pre-k thru the fifth grade made posters. When Daddy walked down the halls, the kids lined up and waved flags and wiggled their posters at him. Abby's class stayed inside their classroom, but they could hear the noise out in the hall and probably Abby was wondering what was going on. Momma said when Daddy went into Abby's room, she jumped up and ran to him. Granny Pat said she thought Abby was coming over to hug her, but she was wrong! Abby walked around Granny Pat and got her backpack off the hook on the wall and headed straight to the door. She didn't even stop to ask her teacher if it was okay. She was going home with her daddy!

Even outside, all the way to the portable building where I went to class, the kids were lined up and clapping and waving their flags and jiggling their posters. Being at the very end of the line of kids, I didn't know what they were yelling about until I saw my daddy. I jumped straight up and he caught me in his arms and lifted me high up in the sky where his head is. I'd forgotten how tall Daddy was, but really it wasn't that much higher than me. After all, I'd grown a lot taller since he'd been gone. I got to go home with them, too, right at that very minute.

We went to Miss Ronda's house to get Mia. Mia was asleep and didn't appreciate us waking her up and she frowned her terribliest frown at Daddy. Even though Daddy got down real low beside where she was sleeping, she still looked a little scared of him. I remembered the first time he came back from war and all I wanted to do was hold onto Momma's leg so he wouldn't grab me and pick me up. But, back then I was real little and afraid of going so high up in the sky. Probably that was why Mia acted like she did, too.

Finally, Daddy asked her if she would let him pick her up and she nodded. He gently slipped his arms under her and eased her up into the air until I could see her eyes peeping at me over his shoulder. They looked really big—like she was scared but by the time we all got buckled into our car seats, she was smiling. Probably she wasn't too scared of Daddy since I was right there to protect her. It was probably a good thing Daddy didn't go get her before they came to my school to get me.

Granny Pat took all the posters and taped them inside the big windows of the old Western store next to the library. With the porch light shining on the posters each night, the whole town of Florence could read about my daddy coming home from war. Granny Pat said it was good for other people to share in being thankful that he got home safely, especially since a lot of those same people had been praying for him and my family since he'd had to go back to Iraq. God likes people to pray and He really likes it when you tell Him thank you that He answered your prayers. That made me stop and think about the pilgrims. I bet they told God thank you at least a dozen hundred times that the Indians didn't eat them for Thanksgiving dinner.

I had to toughen up once Daddy got home. He didn't let me whine to Momma about every little bump and cut I got or put up with me crying about having to go to bed at night. Momma, Mia, Abby, and Leah were glad he was home and they took turns hugging him. I was really glad he was home, too, 'cause I got help doing all the manly things I had to do while he was gone, like gathering up the trash and fixin' whatever Mia broke. It was good having another man in the house.

Of course, since he was home, I'd heard more talk about us moving. I wished I could get it figured out in my head how far away next summer was. I asked Abby if she knew, and that made her sit down and draw all the months on separate pieces of paper, and then she drew the four seasons on separate pieces of paper. At first I thought summer was only as far away as the length of time it took Abby to do all the drawings, and I started gathering up my transformers so I wouldn't forget any of them. But Abby said it wouldn't come that quickly. According to her, summer would be the first day after the leaves stopped falling, the snow quit coming down, and the spring flowers started popping up out of the ground. Hmmm, guess it wouldn't hurt to ask God to hold off on the flowers until I got to be nine or twenty-two. I'd probably be ready for an adventure when I got that old. Next time we stopped to say our Dear Lords before we got onto the highway, I'd just pray about that.

Chapter Six

Walking Your Pig

Grownups were funny! Granny Pat warned me that I better not lie or the bottoms of my feet would turn black and everyone would know I was guilty. But, then she and Momma and Daddy kept our moving to El Paso a secret from us kids. Wasn't that a lie? Well, I kinda hoped it wasn't 'cause lying was one of the ways you end up having to go to the hot water and live with the Devil, and I really didn't want anyone in my family to do that!

Finally, Momma and Daddy told us kids that we would be moving to El Paso. They said we would live on the army base and have neighbors right next door. I could take all my transformers and me and Mia could take all our guns, even though they didn't shoot real bullets and we'd have to tell the neighbors so they wouldn't be scared of us. I didn't know how Momma would find a suitcase big enough for Abby to take all of her Barbie dolls, but I could tell you right now, Abby wouldn't leave even one of them behind.

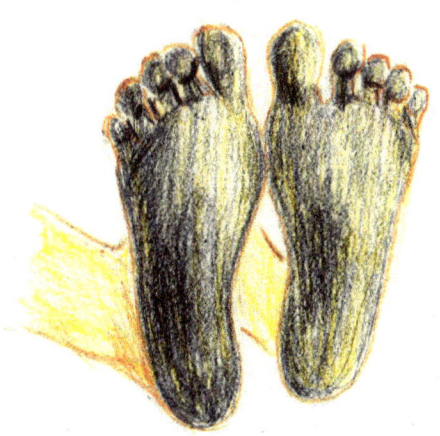

But Granny Pat and Grandpa couldn't go. Granny Pat said they could come and visit us a lot in El Paso. I'd miss them, but wouldn't miss old Sarge 'cause he was always tripping me up and trying to steal my shoes. And, if the army base had lots of swing sets and things to play on, I wouldn't miss our playground here at the ranch. I was getting kind of tired of doing the same thing anyway.

Kiki and Granddaddy came the week before Christmas to see Daddy and to bring us our gifts. School was out and we all played really hard each day. Santa Claus came to our house and left us a huge pile of toys. Mia liked my toys better than hers and we spent most of the holidays shooting each other with play guns. I didn't like to fall down and play dead because it hurt, so Mia did it mostly. Big brothers were much smarter than little sisters and I could easily persuade her to do all the hurting things.

When we were in Granny Pat's van, she drove us through a neighborhood and tried to explain what living in a neighborhood would be like. People were walking and running for exercise and other people were walking their dogs. Mia said people would be walking their pigs and walking their goats in our new neighborhood, and Granny Pat started laughing a lot.

I was afraid Mia wouldn't like it when we moved because she's was little and thought everything would be the same wherever we go. Come to think of it, Abby didn't like change at all. Moving might be kind of loud when we got to El Paso. I was glad Daddy was home 'cause he could get the girls to quit crying a lot faster than I could. Maybe I better rethink growing up and having children. Having dogs might be a lot quieter.

Change would be good . . . I thought.

Chapter Seven
Riding an Elephant

Grandpa took me and Leah to the Monster Truck show. Wow, was it loud, even though we poked these little spongy things in our ears and I wore my gun shootin' ear covers over them. The trucks were really big and they crashed into things and climbed this huge pile of dirt and an ambulance came out and picked one of the drivers up after he turned over. Grandpa bought me a monster truck and Leah a t-shirt, and I was so worn out I slept all the way home. I wanted to be a monster truck driver except for I didn't want to get hurt and have to cry in front of all those people. That would be embarrassing!

Granny Pat took us four kids to the circus. The circus was the greatest thing I'd ever been to except for the elephant rides. Granny Pat made me ride the elephant with Abigail and Mia. Mia wasn't the least bit afraid! She climbed up the stairs to the elephant's back before Granny Pat even got the tickets bought. Abigail went right up behind her and they bunched up

with a bunch of other kids. But I had to ride in the very back because it took me so long to agree to get on. I held on for dear life to both sides of the carrier while the huge thing walked around in a circle. I was so glad it only walked around one time, but Granny Pat said we didn't get our thirty dollars worth. Well, she wouldn't have to worry about spending money on me for another elephant ride because even if went to another circus, and even if they had elephant rides, I was never going to ride another elephant! Never!

There were these two motorcycle riders and they drove around and around inside this monstrous ball that you could see through. They went faster and faster and made lots of noise and didn't even hit each other! Then a lady got inside the ball and they went around and around and they didn't hit her either. It was the coolest thing I'd ever seen. We saw a white tiger and dogs that did tricks and the elephants came out of their pen and rolled around a little. The next coolest thing was this bendy lady that bended up so much, she shot a bow and arrow with her feet. When we got home that night we bended and twisted and put on a circus show for Mom and Dad, but I didn't think we were as good as the bendy lady. I'd have to practice some more to do all her tricks.

I hoped if they had a circus in El Paso that they didn't have any elephants to ride. In a way, though, I was glad Granny Pat made me ride the elephant or Grandpa would have teased me terribly about it! He called me a sissy most of the time anyway. Moving to El Paso might be a good thing. But, no, moving made me sad and Granny Pat said we should stop talking about it. I told her I loved her so much and wanted to stay here on County Line with her even if Grandpa did tease me all the time. I asked if maybe Sarge could go in my place.

She laughed hard and said I knew Grandpa wouldn't give up his old spoiled dog for a whiny grandson, and besides, I had to go with my family. I pouted up and went off into the toy room by myself for a little while, but remembered Grandpa had some good snacks in the cabinet in the kitchen and I went to investigate. While I was eating a green one, I discussed how far it was to El Paso with Granny Pat. First, though, I had to figure out in my little head how far it was to Iraq.

I thought it was about a hundred steps to Iraq because Daddy was gone so long to war. And about twenty steps to Granddaddy and KiKi's house in Tennessee because they couldn't come very often and it took us a zillion years to drive there. I said that probably made it about thirteen steps to El Paso, but Granny Pat said more like ten as she could drive it in one day. So I thought that meant she could come see us a lot more times than KiKi and Granddaddy could.

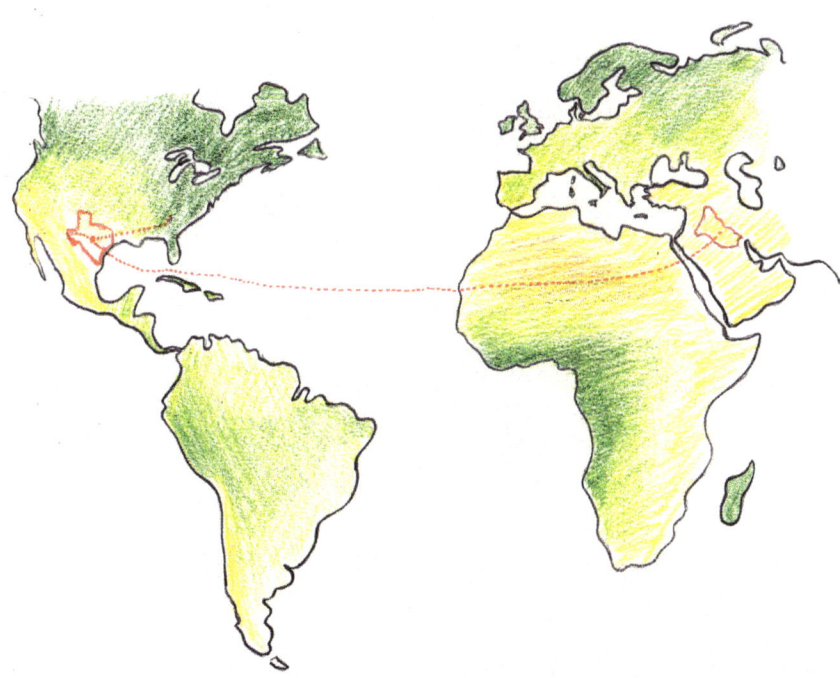

But Granny Pat would have to have a new car first. The one she had was broken. If you wanted to listen to "I want a hippopotamus for Christmas" or "Grandma got runned over by a reindeer," then you had to use tweezers to push in the CD and then use them to pull it out. It was very hard for Granny Pat to make it work, and she wouldn't do it while driving, so we had to pull over and pray about it. We'd learned that we should pray when she got out the tweezers instead of waiting until she gave up trying, because the CD where the frogs were croaking was all scratched up on the edges from the tweezers. But it was soooo funny when the CD got stuck—it sounded like the frogs were burping! Maybe a new van wouldn't be as much as fun as her old van. I'd ask God what He thought about it the next time I said my Dear Lords.

Chapter Eight
In Search of a Mystery

Since I was so grown up now, and I hardly ever whined anymore, and Granny Pat had a three-day weekend 'cause the bank had a holiday, she said it was time I started searching for my mystery on the ranch. I had to be old enough to understand that I could never go off exploring by myself because of the mean cows and the three deep tanks of water on the ranch. Plus, I had to be old enough to remember that if I ever got lost, or if I had to go to the house because Granny Pat got hurt by a rattlesnake or fell and hurt her body, that I should go to the closest fence and follow it to one of the four houses on the ranch. I learned both of those rules really quick and she and I packed a bag with stuff we might need like water, chapstick, and a camera. We left the house without our coats, but had to come back after we got to the first water tank as it was cold down near the water. Then we put on our caps, gloves, and coats and left again.

    I had the bestest time discovering things. Did you know that there was a rock out in the first pasture that looked just like the controller on our video games? And I found lots of Indian ears, they were everywhere, but I didn't find a single cowboy heart. I guess that explained why there were still lots of cowboys in Texas. Poor Indians. They should have had badder arrows that could have killed more cowboys.

That first day we discovered where an old cowboy house used to be. There was a snuff bottle and barrel rim lying right on the ground. Granny Pat took lots of pictures of me at the cowboy house to use in my mystery. Then the next day, Mia went with us, and we drove Grandpa's Ranger. We discovered trees near the cowboy house that had at one time been strung with three strands of wire. The trees had grown up taller so it looked like the old wire pens were really tall. I thought maybe the cowboys kept giraffes in the pens or maybe grown bears, but Granny Pat said no way. Granny Pat had to carry Mia half of the time 'cause I didn't know why. We kept asking Mia why she wanted to be carried, but she said it was pecause she just did. I think she got scared and didn't want to tell us when we were talking about what kind of animal used its long claws to scratch in the mud. Mia acted like she was a tough cowboy, always making her voice real deep when she talked, but she was really a sissy baby girl! But don't tell her I said that 'cause she'd whack me with something, and then start crying first, like she was sorry she accidentally hit me. Sometimes I thought she might possibly be smarter than I was.

While Granny Pat was holding Mia, I hollered, "Look at me!" I was hanging upside down, my legs and arms wrapped around a leaning oak tree, acting like a monkey. As Granny Pat was pulling out her camera to get my picture, we heard this noise and the whole tree came out of the ground and fell on me! The tree had me pinned down on the ground, the trunk on my chest and my face right in the open part between two big limbs. Granny Pat dumped Mia on the ground and she moved the tree off me. I cried a little 'cause my face and chest hurt, but then Granny Pat pointed out how strong I was to rip a whole oak tree out of the ground by its roots! Wow! I must be strong! Grandpa should be impressed and stop calling me a whiny baby!

Me and Granny Pat went back one more time to the cowboy site and pulled logs and sticks around to make walls for a house. Then we stacked up sticks and put rocks around it like it was a fireplace. I was real pleased with the way it looked after all our hard work, but I was pretty well worn out. Granny Pat said my tail was dragging when we got back to the house, and she was right. I was kinda glad I had to go back to school the next day 'cause discovering things was pretty hard work. Maybe when I got to be a trillion years old like Granny Pat was, I'd be able to walk all over the ranch and not want to ride in the Ranger to make discoveries.

My big sister, Leah, said she tells God thank you that our other grandma, Kiki, was such a good cook. But we don't have to remember to say that about Granny Pat 'cause her cooking wasn't too great. But, I was thankful she liked to write each one of us grandchildren a mystery 'cause it was fun searching for discoveries. As Mia would say, I wuv Granny Pat pecause she's fun. I need to remember to tell God about Granny Pat. Maybe He could do something about her cooking.

Chapter Nine

Acting Out Plays & Riding in the Magic Bus

I'd grown up so much this year that Abby thought I could read! In the middle of the Easter play we were doing in Granny Pat's garage, I forgot my lines. Abby handed me the script to read and Mom had to tell her that I couldn't read. But, I did know my letters. Mia was better at sounding out the letters than I was, but she didn't really know that frog starts with an F. She just mimicked whatever I said.

You should have heard what Mia said in the middle of our "God Is Love" play that we did for Valentine's. It was a good thing we didn't put on the play inside of Lawler Baptist Church like we did last Easter or Brother Roy would have been mad at Granny Pat. But, really, it wasn't Granny Pat's fault that Mia made her voice real deep and said, "I love a cowboy. He's gonna come home and hug me." She stomped her little boots like he was walking across our board front porch and she said, "He's gonna hug me." And then in her deepest voice ever she added, "In his underwear."

I was laughing so hard I nearly fell down and Mom, Dad, Grandpa, and Leah covered their mouths and tried hard not to giggle. Granny Pat just stood there with her mouth open 'cause she couldn't believe Mia just said that on camera and right in the middle of a play about God!

So before we did our "Jesus is Risen" play this Easter, Granny Pat had a talk with the three of us. Even though we were supposed to be stuffed animals sitting on the shelves in our Sunday school rooms at Lawler Baptist Church, Granny Pat didn't want to take any chances that Mia could come up with another cowboy in-his-underwear line. We did okay, even though Mia kept waving at everyone and asking who was supposed to be sitting in the empty chair.

I was a skunk and I wore a skunk cape that Granny Pat made me, and I got to show the audience how I would have sprayed the bad men that took

Jesus to be crucified. Mia was a soft baby deer and she kept leaving us and running out into the audience to butt the bad guys with her horns. Abby was a soft pink rabbit and she played her part just perfect. Abby's really good at playing parts 'cause she watches so many movies. I bet she grows up to be either a real princess or an actress in lots of plays.

I hoped that Granny Pat could come up with a different story for Easter next year. She and Brother Roy told us the same story for two years about Jesus dying and then rising from the dead. I asked Granny Pat during Brother Roy's sermon why Brother Roy always talked about God when we were at church. Couldn't he tell a different story once in awhile? Granny Pat laughed and said she was happy that I paid enough attention at church to know that Brother Roy always mentioned that Jesus died for our sins. Brother Roy told me that it was his job to talk about God each Sunday. Okay. That was all right with me, but I just wished once in awhile he could add something about dinosaurs or wild animals. I might not get so wiggly if he did.

Granny Pat said she was worried about us missing Sunday school when we moved to El Paso. She hoped Momma and Daddy would find a good church and take us with them. She said she was going to come out to El Paso and check on us often. She and Grandpa bought this big camper with lots of seats and a motor in the front where you drive it. Grandpa had a bedroom in the back so he couldn't hear us kids in the front, and it had lots of places for us grandkids to spend the night. It had steps that when you opened the door, they came right out like magic so you could hop on board, so I named it the magic bus. I was thinking that maybe Granny Pat could bring our teachers Miss Mindy, Miss Pat, Jo Jo, and Jason with

her so we could have Sunday school at our new house. It was big enough to hold everybody. I bet she could even cram Brother Roy and Miss Mary in it, too, if Brother Roy could think of any new stories to bring with him. Maybe, if he had the time, he could pray about it!

Chapter Ten
Playing Baseball & Hunting Deer Antlers

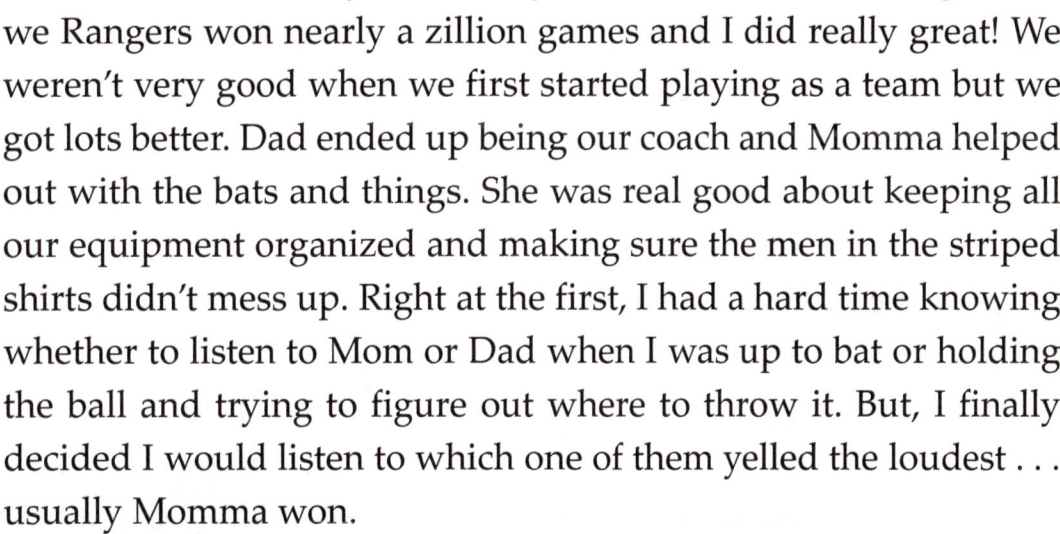

Time was running out. It was getting closer and closer to when we were moving to El Paso. Momma said to quit worrying her about moving until after I finished all my baseball games. Well, I was through, and we Rangers won nearly a zillion games and I did really great! We weren't very good when we first started playing as a team but we got lots better. Dad ended up being our coach and Momma helped out with the bats and things. She was real good about keeping all our equipment organized and making sure the men in the striped shirts didn't mess up. Right at the first, I had a hard time knowing whether to listen to Mom or Dad when I was up to bat or holding the ball and trying to figure out where to throw it. But, I finally decided I would listen to which one of them yelled the loudest . . . usually Momma won.

I liked baseball and told Momma that I wanted to play a few more games. One of the reasons I wanted to play some more was because I was nervous about moving to El Paso, and that way I could put off moving for a while longer. This whole thing about leaving Grandpa, Granny Pat, and Sarge was worrying me. How were they supposed to get along if I wasn't here to help out? Just this morning Granny Pat asked me to run into her house and tell Grandpa a message, and yesterday Grandpa needed me and Mia to go out in the pasture with him and look for deer-antler sheds. And we found one!

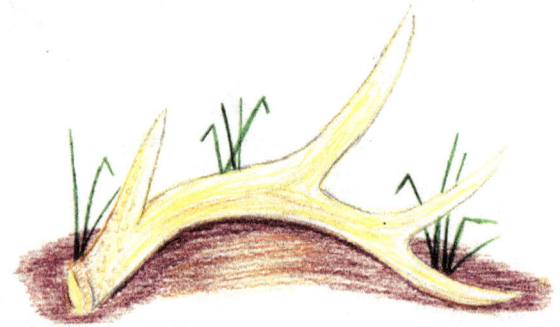

Granny Pat was babysitting us last night while Mom and Dad went to a dress-up ball. She wouldn't let me take the shed I found into my bedroom 'cause she said one of the four points might poke somebody since deer antlers were pretty sharp. I finally agreed to let her put them up high over the television cabinet so Mia couldn't get hurt on them. They looked pretty cool up there. I guessed when we moved to El Paso I could bring my new friends into our new house and show them the shed. Explaining to town kids about how deer get new antlers each year might be kind of hard, but I'd give it a try. Grandpa said that town kids are pretty dumb about the things that really matter in life, like deer getting new antlers and why it was so important to shut a gate if you were the one who opened it.

Momma's friend who lived in El Paso took a picture of our new house. It had bricks on the outside and a sidewalk that ran right beside the paved street. We also had a fire hydrant for the firemen to use in case we had a fire. Grandpa said Sarge would really like to live in a house that had a fire hydrant but I didn't understand why . . . Sarge didn't ever put out any fires.

Momma said there was a playground right beside our house! Abby was gonna love that because she loved to swing and swing and swing some more. I hoped the playground had some green grass because our yard was only rocks! Mia would be tickled 'cause she loved to throw rocks. But, I just bet they had rules in El Paso about kids throwing rocks 'cause if they didn't, a lot of town kids would get hurt by us country kids. Anybody knew we could throw rocks better than anyone.

I curled up beside Granny Pat's big body and just hugged her last night. I told her I liked her just the way she was and that she shouldn't pay any attention to Mia when she kept on asking Granny Pat why she ate so much butter. Grandpa had a big stomach, but his was mainly from popcorn 'cause he'd eaten popcorn every day for millions of years. Sarge was fat, too, but he didn't eat popcorn or butter. He was fat because Grandpa gave him canned dog food, people cookies, and cut up weenies

every time he fed him. If the three of them didn't stop growing, they might not be able to fit into the magic bus and never get to come see us in El Paso. Come to think of it, maybe I better just pray about that. . . .

Chapter Eleven
Talking to Dear Lord

Abby was crazy about Sea World. Ever since we went there on Spring Break, she'd been talking about being a whale trainer when she grew up. When Mom let her on the computer, she went straight to Google and typed in whales. I bet she'd looked at every whale site in the world and she was only nine years old. And, Abby could remember everything she read! I could kind of understand if she was that interested in football or maybe baseball, but not whales. She had to stop before she made my head pop!

Yesterday on the way to church, we stopped to say our "Dear Lords." Abby said, "And please let me learn about whales and be a whale trainer." Well, really we just slowed down and pulled out on the highway and kept on praying because it took us all so long to tell God what we wanted to tell him that we would be late for Sunday school or Florence's Buffalo school.

Anyway, Mia said the funniest prayer: "Dear Lord, thank you for all my sins." I started to correct her but Granny Pat said not to because God knew what she meant to say because he could see into our hearts.

I said, "And thank you that Sarge didn't kill the chicken," because Sarge had one of the hens pinned to the ground and was trying to bite her head off when we left the ranch. But Granny Pat rolled down her window and yelled at him until he turned the hen loose. Everyone on the ranch listened when Granny Pat yelled at you . . . She was pretty scary sometimes...

At church Abby insisted that Granny Pat tear out all the pages that Abby had already drawn on in her blue notebook. Abby started a "Whale" notebook . . . the first page said, "Believe." I wasn't real sure what she meant by that except for maybe she wanted you to believe that her drawings were whales. They did sorta look like whales. Anyway, while she was drawing she told Granny Pat that Abby wanted to be a trainer at Sea World when she grew up (as if Granny Pat didn't already know this). And then Abby said, "Like you're a pink ribbon."

Granny Pat gave her a quizzical look and shushed her until there was a break in the singing. "What do you mean I'm a pink ribbon?"

Abby said, "Like at your desk. At work. You are a pink ribbon!"

I could see Granny Pat trying to figure out what Abby meant and then after church she asked her about it one more time. "You mean, at my job, I'm a pink ribbon?"

Abby said, "Yes!" in a very loud voice, as if we were all dumb or something.

Come to think of it, Granny Pat did have a lot of pink ribbons around her desk. And I knew her favorite color was pink because Abby asked her a thousand hundred times, "What's your favorite color, Granny Pat?" So I guess Abby was right, Granny Pat's job was a pink ribbon. It must be a good job because Granny Pat loved to go to work. I'd heard her tell Grandpa several times that she was glad she had a job to go to. It must be she hated to clean house, because I knew she loved keeping us three little pigs all the time!

But back to Abby. Somebody better find something else for her to think about because I heard Momma talking to Daddy about what happened last night. Daddy got out of bed because he saw a light on in the living room and went to turn it off. He went around the corner to check on Abby and bumped into her coming out of her room. She was hiding something and he made her show it to him. It was her suitcase, and it had a sleeping bag and her bathing suit inside it. Abby had also written a letter to our family that said she was going to Sea World to be a trainer and she'd be back by the 18th to go to school. I bet if it hadn't been so dark outside, and ol' Sarge hadn't been sleeping on our front porch, Abby would have made it off the ranch and onto the highway before anyone missed her.

If I had pulled that stunt my bottom would be red all the way to next Christmas. (I learned that sayin' from Grandpa.) Like I said, somebody better come up with something else for Abby to think about or she'd pack her stuff up again and hit the road on her scooter.

You know, I'm worried about us moving to El Paso. What if Abby wanted to come home to be closer to Sea World and slipped out of the house with her suitcase? Granny Pat said there were street lights in El Paso and Sarge wasn't moving with us so Abby could run away real easily. No matter how crazy she made me by repeating everything over and over again, we didn't want to lose Abby way off on the outskirts of Texas.

Maybe I better ask our family of friends at Lawler Baptist Church to pray about that . . . .

Chapter Twelve

Three Little Pigs on the 4th of July

We'd been busy this summer since school was out and Leah graduated, so I hadn't had much time to think about movin' or prayin.' Granny Pat always stopped before we got onto the highway on the way to school so we could say our Dear Lords, which made us think about God right at the start of our busy day. Maybe during the summer I should stop and say Dear Lords when I climbed down out of my bed, before Mia and I start fighting over toys or who was going to be first at something.

Right after school was out, our family went to Disney World and we met Granddaddy and Kiki. We got to stay five whole days and see lots of cool things. On the way back to County Line, Abby wrote down a list of which park each one of us liked the most. I thought Abby would get stuck on princesses again after seeing so many of them walking around Disney World, but she came home still talking about being a whale trainer.

Then Granny Pat and Grandpa went on a trip and they were gone eight days,

which seemed like forever. She brought back each of us a t-shirt that says, "This little pig went to market," because she calls us her three little pigs.

We were going to do one more play before we moved to El Paso as soon as Granny Pat could find us some bricks. We had plenty of sticks and hay on the ranch to build the other two houses. Granny Pat said she would add a part about the three little pigs saying their Dear Lords so we could get some more stickers to go in our witnessing books. She wanted to make sure we three little pigs weren't afraid to talk about Jesus before we moved to El Paso in case they didn't know about him out there. I wasn't afraid to talk about God and Jesus, but I was worried about Mia. She thought cowboys were right up there with God and Jesus, so we had to work on getting her straightened out before we moved.

We were moving in July and here it was already July! I had a lot of things to get settled before we left the ranch. One thing that was really worrying me was who was gonna take care of Grandpa when we left. He was always getting hurt, like breaking his little finger or dropping a tractor part on his toe. Since Granny Pat got all wavy whenever she saw him hurt, my momma had to doctor him up and make him all better.

And, Sarge had been acting crazy. Granny Pat said this morning that Sarge must have gotten bitten by a rabbit since he went around eating grass and nibbling on tree leaves. Grandpa took him to the doctor two times because Sarge kept crying about his long tail hurting. Grandpa gave him medicine every day, but Sarge was not getting any better. I worried he'd die after we left because he'd miss us three kids so much and his tail hurt him. Plus, I worried about Granny Pat. How was she gonna survive without us kids to talk to and pick up at Ms. Ronda's every day? Momma told me to quit worrying about Granny Pat! She said she would be just fine. At least Grandpa didn't tease Granny Pat the way he did us kids 'cause she'd take her yellow flyswatter to him if he did.

Yesterday was the 4th of July. We went to the park in Georgetown. We rode the ponies and a lot of other rides and went to the petting zoo. Then last night we went out to Andice to play and see the fireworks. We had the bestest time ever, even though the fireworks were really loud and we had to cover up our ears. I had a flag painted on my face. Abby got a real pretty flower. Mia wanted a curly black moustache and she got one. I laughed my head off looking at her. I bet if they could of drawn on guns and chaps, she would have let 'em.

Granny Pat smiled big all day and night. I asked her why she was so happy and she said it was because my daddy was home with us this year. She said she never really enjoyed celebrating the 4th of July when he was overseas fighting a war.

I enjoyed him being home, too, 'cause he and another soldier daddy played with us kids before the fireworks started. I overheard her and Momma talking about where we would be next year on the 4th of July. Daddy would be through with Sgt. Major School and we might be moving to some place new. I sure hoped Daddy would get to be there with us again. I agreed with Granny Pat, it was much more fun to have your daddy home on the 4th of July. Was it too early to start praying about that?

Chapter Thirteen
Leaving County Line Ranch

Thirteen was my Granny Pat's lucky number so I was pretty sure I'd stop writing after this chapter. Everything that needed to be said had been said, and my true personality at five years old was captured on paper. It was like one of Abby's drawings where she made me look like a cowboy. Only Granny Pat helped draw what I looked like with words. When I got bigger and learned how to read, I was gonna write a really scary story about dinosaurs, snakes, and bears, since those were the scariest things I knew about. But, if it took too much time to write, I'd just skip it and go straight to being a fireman or a policeman.

by T. Williams

Momma and Daddy were cleaning out our house, getting ready for the movers to come on July 25th. For a few nights we would move into Granny Pat's house until we left on July 28th. Daddy was worried about Leah 'cause he thought she would have a hard time going off and leaving her boyfriend, Kameron. I liked Kameron, too, but everybody said Leah could make new friends in El Paso. It might be harder for her to find one to kiss on, but I really didn't know much about that.

Before we left, Granny Pat and Grandpa were taking us in the magic bus for our fourth trip. Abby was so excited because she liked for things to keep going and going and going. She'd been bugging Granny Pat about when we'd go on our fourth adventure so she could add more pictures to our Magic Bus book. We were going to a place called Jellystone where they had swimming pools and fun stuff for kids.

You know, Granny Pat had been working with us on our three little pigs' play that we were going to put on for the whole family before we moved. Mia nearly cracked us up when we stopped to say our Dear Lords on Sunday morning. She said, "Dear Lord, thank you that the big bad wolf can't blow down our little pigs' house made out of bricks."

I burst out laughing really hard, but Granny Pat made me stop. Granny Pat had a talk with me after church about my not wanting to say my Dear Lords. I told her I'd already said them a dozen times and it was really boring. She reminded me that when we left for church, I was upset because I didn't get to hug my momma and daddy goodbye. Granny Pat said God liked for us to hug Him, too, every morning and that I should remember how good a hug feels next time I don't want to say my Dear Lords. After all He is our Father in heaven and we are His kids.

I kind of hung my head and acted sad, but Granny Pat hugged me and said my not understanding about needing to pray every day was no worse than Mia praying about the big bad wolf. Everybody had a lot to learn about saying their Dear Lords.

Then she told me about when she was little. Her grandpa Bob used to end each of his prayers with "and K-nay-da bless us. Amen." So she started saying and K-nay-da bless us at the end of her prayers at night. When she got older, she read all the Bible story books that her grandma Flossie had on the bookshelves and she didn't find anyone named K-nay-da in the books. Finally, she talked to her mother about it, and her mother couldn't figure out what she was talking about. So the next time they ate Sunday dinner with Grandpa Bob, her momma listened real good to what he said at the end. (It was so funny!) What he really said was "and continue to bless us. Amen." Granny Pat said that even though she said the wrong thing at the end of her prayers for a zillion nights, God knew what she meant and didn't get mad that she had it wrong. And I was glad, and I was going to quit worrying about Mia not gettin' to go up to heaven and going down to the hot water. Abby worried about it enough for the both of us, anyway.

I was born going to Lawler, and so was Mia. I loved Jason and Jo Jo and Miss Mindy and the other ladies who helped out with the little kids. I wouldn't get to stay at Lawler until I was old enough to go to Miss Pat's class like Abby. Abby got to carry her Bible with the pink princess case to Sunday school class and she was gettin' real good about writing down Bible verses. Now that I was too old to stay in the nursery during Brother Roy's time to talk, I'd admit I wasn't too crazy about having to be still for an hour. But, Granny Pat said it was good for us to be in church together. We'd even started sitting beside Grandpa, and he behaved better than he used to. Maybe he was finally growing up!

I'd grown up a lot since I first found out we were moving to El Paso. I wasn't scared anymore to go. It was time for me to tell everyone goodbye and to thank all my family at Lawler for taking care of us three little pigs. Granny Pat said that when Abby was just three years old and first started coming to Lawler that she couldn't hear very well at all, and didn't want to be around all the people. And that Abby would sit *under* the table at dinner on the grounds. Granny Pat would feed her Miss Mary's chicken and rice while she sat on the floor. Gradually, Abby got used to all the people and all the loud noise. Everyone prayed a lot for her and she got these little tiny hearing aids and started hearing better. And then, when I came along to go with her, Abby started eating at the table with me. (But it makes me wonder if that was why they started calling it dinner on the ground because of Abby sitting under the table?) We were going to miss Miss Mary's chicken and rice and all the other ladies' really good desserts. Maybe our momma would learn to cook desserts like the Lawler ladies while we lived in El Paso. Was it all right to pray about that?

We'd be back to visit. But in the meantime, maybe Lawler should get a yellow fly swatter so they could swat Grandpa and Granny Pat if they seemed too sad. Remind them that God was watching to see if they acted up at Sunday school or church, so they better be really good. Granny Pat said she would pray that our parents found a church that would love us like Lawler did.

I hoped we weren't so grown up next time Lawler got to see us that they didn't recognize us. I figured I'd grow up taller than Abby and look like her big brother one of these days. I hoped Mia hadn't turned completely into a cowboy by then.

As long as our daddy was brave enough to be in the Army and fight for our freedom, we three little pigs should be brave enough to move from base to base. But, no matter how much we liked El Paso, County Line Ranch would always be my favorite place to say my Dear Lords at night.

The real kids of Thomas' Little Light

Kids in their little pig shirts

Mia

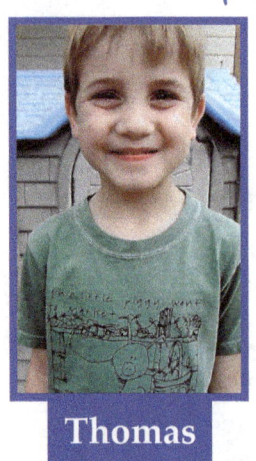
Thomas

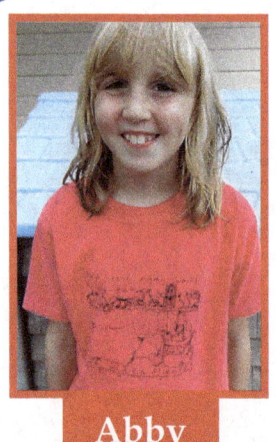
Abby

All 3 kids

Walking to church

Thomas' family

Thomas with Sarge

Kids with pigs

Plays

God Is Love

The Three Little Pigs

Jesus Is Risen

Saving the Royal Baby from Rumpus the Dinosaur

Patricia Rodgers was born in central Texas and grew up in a family of storytellers. Remembering how special she felt as a child weaving her own name into an adventure story, Patricia began composing a story for each of her grandchildren. This trilogy shows the way three children from the same military family handle their father's deployments to foreign lands and the necessary moves from one military base to another. Rodgers believes the most important part of growing up is learning to accept that God is always beside you.

Romy Vekony lived in Tucson, Arizona for most of her life and is now a senior philosophy major and art minor at Covenant College in Lookout Mountain, Georgia. She enjoys running, writing, and drawing in her spare time. She is fascinated by science and nature and hopes to continue her education about God's world as long as she can.

CPSIA information can be obtained
at www.ICGtesting.com
Printed in the USA
LVHW020821240723
752989LV00010B/305